Heroes of the American Revolution

Text by David Brownell

Engravings by Alonzo Chappel and drawings by Nancy Conkle

General Washington, on the front cover, is by John Trumbull, The Henry Francis du Pont Winterthur Museum

General George Washington *

When on June 15, 1775 Congress chose 43-year-old George Washington of Virginia "to command all the Continental forces raised or to be raised for the defence of American liberty," Washington did not want the job. He had no love for war, though he had served with distinction for 5 years in the French and Indian War, and he had hoped that a war between Britain and the colonies would not be necessary. Never having commanded an army, he doubted his own ability, and called this job "too boundless for my abilities and far, very far beyond my experience." He was conscious that as military leader of a rebellion against Britain he would be the first to be executed for treason if the rebellion failed. And at the beginning of the war the colonial cause looked unpromising to Washington. Americans faced the most powerful nation in Europe, with ample supplies of money, soldiers, and ships. America lacked all these. Unlike many others Washington expected no easy victory. All he could foresee was "a struggle protracted, dubious, and savage."

And what could he offer to the struggle? "I can answer but for three things: a firm belief in the justice of our cause, close attention to the prosecution of it, and the strictest integrity. If these cannot supply the place of ability and experience, the cause will suffer, and more than probable my character along with it." To indicate that he accepted his position to serve the cause, not his own interests, Washington refused a salary, and asked only that his expenses be paid.

Congress chose Washington because he had more military experience than any other American so committed to the patriot cause; because a Virginian in command of a New England army would symbolize the unity of the colonial cause and draw southern support, and because, while Washington had not said much as a delegate to the Congress, he impressed people. Over 6 feet tall, he was powerful in body. He was quiet and courteous, with a charm of manner. People who worked with him throughout his life said that he was not quick-thinking or brilliant; when facing a problem, he considered it carefully, avoiding a hasty decision. Before he made his mind up, he usually managed to see and state clearly the essential points of the problem; then he decided the right answer — if there was an answer.

Often there was no answer to Washington's problems. He was making war in a country most of whose inhabitants were not willing to sacrifice their own interests for the cause. The only government was a congress with no real powers, which failed to supply Washington with troops, weapons, supplies, or money. Washington recognized that the war was a means, not an end, and resisted the appeals of those who wanted him to make war more efficiently by taking over command of the government or terrorizing civilians. He recognized that legislatures are slow and disorderly, and remained patient with Congress's inefficiency.

His background as an American helped him in fighting under conditions that would have driven any European-trained general mad. A Virginia planter had to order equipment all the way from England: when something vital was not on the ship, then you had to figure out another way of solving your problem. Washington had the American gift for improvisation.

One thing he had to improvise was an army. He started with a mass of untrained officers and men, and since most men refused to serve more than a year, he had to recreate his army annually.

* on the front cover

He also had to make himself into a general. He read books on the art of war, questioned more expert soldiers, and slowly learned by experience how best to use the talents of an American army. His natural inclination was to fight: he liked to lead his army from the front lines, and was often under fire. But experience taught him to restrain his combativeness in the interests of the cause. He wrote Lafayette, who was always eager to fight, "We must consult our means rather than our wishes; and not endeavor to better our affairs by attempting things which for want of success may make them worse."

As a general he learned from experience. In the campaigns around New York he made several disastrous errors, but he never repeated them. He came to see that his greatest assets were the superior mobility of American troops, which allowed the use of hit-and-run tactics, and their superior devotion to their cause, which made them willing to endure great hardships when necessary. He used both these assets at the end of 1776, when the American cause appeared to be sinking. Washington himself wrote that without reinforcements "I think the game is pretty near up." But when the British stopped campaigning and settled their troops in winter quarters scattered through New York and New Jersey, Washington had the audacity to risk a winter campaign. He chanced having his men trapped while crossing an icy river, and his shoeless men left bloody footprints in the snow; but Washington achieved surprise, and won victories at Trenton and Princeton which showed that the American cause was not dead. Washington's firmess made him the embodiment of the American cause, capable of holding together an army without food, supplies, or pay.

At the end of the war Washington astonished mankind by doing what few men had ever done — abandoning power to retire to private life. From Mount Vernon he wrote Lafayette, "I am not only retired from all public employments, but I am retiring within myself, and shall be able to view the solitary walk and tread the paths of private life with heartfelt satisfaction. Envious of none, I am determined to be pleased with all, and this, my dear friend, being the order for my march, I will move gently down the stream of life until I sleep with my fathers."

He was not able to do as he wished: his country's need brought him back to preside over the Constitutional Convention. The Constitution gave powers to the president which its members might not have trusted any man but Washington to use with restraint. Washington again set an example to the world by giving up the presidency after two terms to retire to Mount Vernon, where he died in 1799. In his will he set an example to his neighbors by freeing his slaves.

He was not by nature a great general, but something more important — a great man. Military glory was never an end for him. "How pitiful in the eyes of reason and ambition is that false ambition which desolates the world with fire and sword for the purposes of conquest and fame, when compared to the milder virtues of making our neighbors and our fellow men as happy as their frail conditions and perishable natures permit *them to be*," he said.

The Alfred

Commodore Esek Hopkins

Esek Hopkins was the first commodore of the infant American navy. In the early part of the war the navy's main job was to intercept supplies being shipped to the British troops: each ship captured supplied the Americans with desperately needed equipment while denying the supplies to the British. In February, 1776, Hopkins left the Delaware with a squadron of 5 small ships. His first lieutenant was John Paul Jones. They cruised off Virginia against a British fleet there. Hopkins then decided to attack the Bahamas, a British supply center. He captured Nassau, and seized a number of supplies. On his return voyage he captured 3 British ships off Long Island, but when he returned to port he was censured by Congress for disobeying their orders to "annoy the enemy's ships off the Southern states" and he was dismissed from the navy.

General John Stark

Like many other New Hampshiremen, John Stark was a fiercely independent man who liked to do things his own way. Born in New Hampshire in 1728, he had military experience before the Revolution. In 1753 he had been a prisoner of the Indians (he was ransomed for $103), and during the French and Indian Wars, he was a captain in Robert Rogers's Rangers, a tough force of colonial scouts. He helped capture Ticonderoga in 1756, and saved Fort William Henry from a French attack by managing to keep his Irish soldiers from getting drunk on St. Patrick's Day.

When Stark heard the news of Lexington and Concord, he got his New Hampshire militia down to Boston within 3 days. New Hampshire made him a colonel; at the last moment before the British attack, Stark's regiment was ordered to join the American forces on Breed's Hill. Stark's men paused to melt down lead for their bullets, then marched 4 miles to Charlestown. Stark led them at a slow march through enemy fire to Breed's Hill; when an officer asked whether they could hurry to get out of range, Stark told him, "Dearborn, one fresh man in action is worth ten fatigued men." Stark's men held the American left — a stone wall on the beach — against all attacks, and retreated in good order.

In 1776 Stark went to Canada, to help the American army which retreated after Montgomery's death. By December he was with Washington at the battles of Trenton and Princeton. But when subordinate officers were made brigadiers by Congress in April, 1777, and Stark was not promoted, he resigned in disgust, and went back to New Hampshire.

STARK

Major General Henry Knox

In one of the spectacular feats of the war, Henry Knox, Washington's 280-pound commander of artillery, brought Washington the guns the army needed. Then with quiet competence he trained the men to use his guns — a job requiring technical knowledge — and made the American artillery-men more skillful than the British, and the proudest part of the American army.

Born in Boston in 1750, Knox worked as a bookseller's apprentice from the age of 9 to support his mother and brother. At 21 he set up his own shop. After reading military history, he joined the Boston militia. When the Continental army besieged Boston, the fat, active young officer who was building earthworks caught Washington's eye. Lieutenant Colonel Knox was put in charge of the artillery — all four guns. It was clear that the British could not be driven out of Boston without the aid of cannon. The only ones available in all the colonies were in upstate New York, at Fort Ticonderoga which Ethan Allen and Benedict Arnold had captured May 10, 1775. But these guns were 250 miles away from Boston, over a range of mountains with no roads. Knox decided to bring Washington those guns. Arriving at Ticonderoga December 5, he selected the best guns there, 43 cannon and 16 mortars, weighing a total of 60 tons. He loaded these onto boats, to move them as far as possible before ice closed the lakes. By December 17 he had all his guns at the end of the lake, though the last boat had to chop a passage through the ice. Since heavy guns in wagons on muddy roads would simply sink into the mud, Knox waited for a freeze. Sleds moving over frozen grounds would work. Knox built sleds, and hired 248 horses. When a freeze came, he loaded his guns and hauled them over the Berkshires, through a mountain pass with no road. By January 27 he and his guns arrived in Boston. When the guns were mounted on Dorchester Heights, they forced the British to evacuate Boston.

Now Knox developed his gunners into a proud and skillful crew. While he wanted Congress to found a national military academy — an idea not carried out till 1802 — Knox was not going to wait for its graduates. He set up his own training school in winter quarters, and lectured himself.

Knox redesigned his carriages so that the artillery could travel as fast as the infantry. In December, 1776, Knox was with Washington when the small American army of 2400 men was ferried across the Delaware by Colonel John Glover's regiment of Marblehead fishermen. Knox supervised the loading of 18 guns, which were safely ferried through the ice floes, and which kept up with the march of the troops that freezing night. When Washington attacked the Hessian troops in Trenton that dawn of December 26, rain kept both sides unable to fire their muskets. But Knox stationed his guns at a commanding crossroad where their fire swept the streets, keeping the German troops from being able to assemble for a bayonet charge. After Trenton, Congress made Knox a brigadier general.

In 1779, when Washington appointed Nathanael Greene to command the southern armies, Greene suggested that the job should be given to Knox: "All obstacles vanish before him; his resources are infinite." "True," said General Washington, "and therefore I cannot spare him."

The final victory for Knox's artillery came at Yorktown, where his guns dominated

HENRY KNOX

the siege. Washington said of Knox in his report to Congress, "The resources of his genius supplied the deficit of means." Congress made Knox a major general.

Knox served as Secretary of War from 1785 to 1794. He was responsible in that period for dealing with the Indians, and tried to see that they were treated fairly. He wanted to make them a part of American society. "It has been conceived impracticable to civilize the Indians of North America. This opinion is probably more convenient than just," he wrote.

When Knox left the cabinet he moved to Maine, where he died in 1806. A cheerful, friendly, patient, inventive man, loved by his associates and always loyal to Washington, Knox was a subordinate any general would be lucky to have.

Major General Israel Putnam

Israel Putnam was heroic, but was not a good general. One of the bravest officers in the American army, Putnam had energy, activity, and perseverence, but he lacked other talents a general needs — foresight, planning powers, and the ability to manage the supplying of his troops.

Putnam made his military reputation at a lower rank in the French and Indian War, where he survived a thousand dangers as a scout. When captured by the Indians he was saved at the last moment from being burned at the stake, once by a timely rainstorm, once by a French officer.

On April 20, 1775, the 57-year-old Putnam heard the news of the battle of Lexington while he was "in leathern frock and apron assisting hired men to build a stone wall" at his farm in Pomfret, Connecticut. Dropping everything, he went off to Boston as he was, arriving next dawn after riding 100 miles in 18 hours. "Old Put," as everyone called him, commanded at Bunker Hill. He seemed to be everywhere at once on the field, trying to get cowards back into battle, rallying wavering troops, demanding reinforcements. After the American defeat Putnam spent the night building a new fort to check any further British advance: he was tireless. When Congress organized the new American army, they made Putnam a major general.

In 1776 the war moved to New York. The British fleet transported an army to attack the city. Putnam was put in command of the American forces on Long Island 3 days before the battle there. Putnam, who did not know the geography of Long Island, left unguarded a pass that led around the American army, and General Howe, the British commander, led his troops through it on a flank march. On August 27 the American troops, taken by surprise, fled in panic. The day was redeemed only by the gallantry of 950 Maryland and Delaware troops under William Alexander, Lord Stirling, one of Washington's best fighting generals. These troops stood off the British army for some time, charging the British to protect the retreat of their fellows. While Putnam was not the only person responsible for the American disaster, he should have guarded the pass, and should not have ignored early reports of the British flank march.

Howe penned Washington's troops up against the harbor on Brooklyn Heights. But under the cover of fog John Glover's regiment of Gloucester fishermen evacuated all the American supplies and all 9500 men from under Howe's nose. Now another American failure followed on Manhattan Island. When the British landed troops at Kip's Bay, halfway up the island, the American soldiers refused to stand and fight. If the British had

ISRAEL PUTNAM

blocked the roads north on the island, they could have cut off half of Washington's troops. But Putnam was at his best in hurrying the retreat of his men, and the Americans got away once again.

After the battles near New York, Putnam served in less demanding posts. His health was not up to field service, so he commanded detachments shielding New England from raids by the British troops in New York. In one such raid, when Putnam's troops were defeated, the old general was chased by British troopers. To escape them he rode his horse at a gallop down a hillside so steep that the troopers were afraid to follow. He died in 1790.

Brigadier General William Moultrie

William Moultrie's moment of glory came in 1776, when a British fleet of 9 vessels under Admiral Sir Peter Parker attacked Charleston. Charleston harbor is shielded by several coastal islands, and on one of these, Sullivan's Island, Moultrie's men built a small fort which became the key to the battle. It was made from two parallel walls of palmetto logs, with sand filling the space between them. A makeshift affair, it only mounted about 30 guns, served by 500 men under Colonel Moultrie; but the British fleet had to pass those guns to get into Charleston harbor.

When the British attacked on June 28, 1776, shot and shells from more than a hundred British guns swept the small fort. 21 American guns bore on the British fleet, and could answer the fire. But the Americans had only 35 rounds of powder for each gun, so they fired slowly, but accurately. The Americans seemed terribly overmatched; but they soon found out that their palmetto wood made a splendid fort; it was soft and spongy, so that cannon balls sank into it without splintering or splitting it. The British fired more often with bigger guns, but the Americans did more damage.

During the battle a British shot broke the fort's flagpole, and the flag fell outside the fort. Sergeant William Jasper climbed over the fort's wall, picked up the fallen flag, attached it to a pole, and stood atop the fort's parapet to remount the flag, as the men cheered him.

When 3 British ships tried to sail past the fort to attack its weakly fortified rear, they went aground on a shoal. One of them was so firmly stuck that its crew had to abandon and burn it. The British gave up their attack at this point, and sailed away. They had lost 64 dead, 131 wounded, to the American's 17 and 20. The British had fired 34,000 pounds of powder, the Americans 4766. And as a final offense to British pride, Admiral Sir Peter Parker suffered a splinter wound in his buttocks.

Moultrie's gallant defense led to his promotion, and his fort was renamed Fort Moultrie. He fought in further battles in the south, and spent two years as a prisoner of war after the British did capture Charleston in 1780. After the war he was several times governor of South Carolina.

Brigadier General William Moultrie

Major General Charles Lee

At the start of the American Revolution, most people thought that Charles Lee would be the greatest American general. He was certainly the most experienced professional soldier available to the cause. Born in Wales in 1731, he was the son of a British officer, and became an army officer himself at 14. Lee fought in America throughout the French and Indian War. He met Washington when they were both part of Braddock's disastrous expedition. For a while Lee lived among the Mohawk Indians with a squaw: the Indians, recognizing Lee's hot temper, called him "Boiling Water." When fighting ended in America, Lee went back to England to find more action. Under General Burgoyne, he led a daring raid in Spain. After this war ended, Lee served the King of Poland. In 1773 he came to live in Virginia, partly because his democratic political views had ruined his chances of rising in the British army.

This experienced soldier, who read and thought a great deal about the art of war, was an odd person; he was described as skinny, ugly, unwashed, and foul-mouthed. He took his dogs everywhere with him; he preferred them to people. Careless in talking and writing, he often said things which got him into trouble. But at the beginning of the war Washington was glad to have the help of a man with so much experience. Lee went to Boston with Washington, and helped lay out the fortifications there. Then he was used as a trouble-shooter, going to different places where British attacks were feared. Wherever the radical Lee went, he preached the necessity of a complete split with England, and did his best to force all men to commit themselves to the American cause.

When a British fleet under Admiral Sir Peter Parker threatened Charleston, Lee was sent there to organize the resistance. Lee struck the leisurely South Carolineans as hasty and rude, but his preparations and William Moultrie's gallant defence of the makeshift fort on Sullivan's Island held off the British attack. Lee returned north covered with glory — one of the few successful American generals. Washington had just lost New York to the British. Various people began to suggest that Lee would make a better commander — an idea that Lee shared. He resisted orders from Washington to unite their troops as Washington retreated across New Jersey; Lee hoped for a chance to act on his own. But when he decided one night to sleep at a comfortable tavern in Basking Ridge, New Jersey, instead of with his troops, he was captured by British cavalry, who carried him off in his bedroom slippers and without his wig.

Lee remained a prisoner for two years, until the Americans captured a British officer of the same rank and could offer a trade. Lee then rejoined Washington; but when they disagreed about the army's tactics at the battle of Monmouth, Lee left the army in disgrace, accused of having been insolent to his commander. He took no further part in the war, and died in 1782.

Major General Philip Schuyler

When Congress appointed the first American generals in June, 1775, the officer they chose to rank second to Washington was Philip Schuyler of New York. Schuyler was born in Albany in 1733, of a Dutch family, and was one of the wealthiest men in the colonies. He had served in the French and Indian War, where he had extensive experience in supplying the armies. Washington assigned Schuyler to command the Northern department — the Canadian frontier. Schuyler, who spoke Mohawk, managed to negotiate an

Major General
Charles Lee

Major General Philip Schuyler

agreement with the Indians that they would remain neutral, and then began to equip an expedition against Canada. When Schuyler fell ill, he let his subordinate Richard Montgomery lead his excursion. Schuyler remained in Albany, making sure that the expedition received needed supplies.

After the Canadian invasion collapsed, Schuyler had to prepare to receive a British invasion from Canada. He recruited new troops while Horatio Gates prepared the army. Schuyler also assigned Benedict Arnold to build a fleet on Lake Champlain, down which the British invasion had to come. The British were forced to build a fleet to match the American one, and were unable to move south down the lake until October, 1776, when their fleet beat Arnold's at the battle of Valcour Island. But by then winter was so close that no further attack could be made that year. Schuyler and Arnold had saved the Americans for a year.

In March, 1777, Congress replaced Schuyler with Gates. The New England troops disliked the rather haughty Schuyler, and even accused him of betraying them to the British. Schuyler answered all charges against him, and was returned to his post, vindicated, in May. He found Fort Ticonderoga too weak to be defended: the British had placed cannon on a mountain which commanded it. Ticonderoga was hastily evacuated. Burgoyne had now come 150 miles south on his journey towards Albany in a few weeks.

Schuyler took hold again, and ordered that Burgoyne be delayed in every possible way. All food was destroyed before the British could capture it. Schuyler burned the crops in his own fields. All bridges were destroyed. Trees were cut down to block the roads. Snipers prowled about the flanks of the advancing British, and killed the men who were working to clear the roads. These tactics worked: it took Burgoyne a month to advance a few miles from Skenesborough to Fort Edward. Meanwhile Schuyler recruited troops and built up the size of his army.

But Congress gave Schuyler's command to Gates August 19 — less than 2 months before Burgoyne surrendered. Gates got the credit for the victory. Schuyler accepted his removal calmly, and gave Gates all the help he could with procuring supplies. He was patriot enough to rejoice at the victory, whoever won it. He resigned from the army, but served Congress in various ways for the rest of the war. After the war he became one of New York's first U.S. Senators. He died in 1801.

Major General Horatio Gates

After Burgoyne's army surrendered to Horatio Gates at Saratoga, October 17, 1777, many patriots thought Gates the greatest of the American generals; but he lost this fame entirely when Cornwallis annihilated his army at Camden, South Carolina, August 16, 1780, in what has been described as "the most disastrous defeat ever inflicted on an American army."

At the start of the American Revolution Gates had perhaps more military experience than any American officer except Charles Lee. Born in 1727, Gates was given a commission in the British army. As a result of a real talent for soldiering he rose to the rank of major during the French and Indian War. He was wounded in Braddock's defeat, and served with distinction at the siege of Martinique. But when peace came, further promotion was blocked. He felt increasing sympathy with the American opposition to the king, and in 1772 he moved to Virginia. At the start of the war, Washington persuaded Congress to make Gates a brigadier general and appoint him adjutant general of the army — the officer in charge of organization and paper-work. Gates did this job very well, and showed several skills beyond paperwork. He was a good housekeeper and disciplinarian for an army.

He was also very good at organizing political support for himself. The radicals in Congress liked Gates's ideas of how to run this war. He favored relying on the militia to fight the British, an idea popular with all those who believed in the traditional English idea that a standing professional army was a standing threat to freedom. Washington, however, argued that, despite this danger, the war could only be won with an army in service long enough to acquire professional training. Congress made Gates a major general in May, 1776.

He was sent to Canada to reorganize the sick and demoralized army that trailed back after Montgomery's death. Under the command of Schuyler, Gates reorganized the army and prepared to withstand the British invasion from Canada. The troops liked the democratic Gates, although they referred to their stooping, elderly-looking general as "Granny Gates," apparently because he fussed so over details.

Gates and Schuyler alternated in command as Congress vacillated. Gates commanded while preparations were made to defend Fort Ticonderoga; Schuyler returned, found the preparations inadequate, and had to evacuate the fort. Shock at this retreat led Congress to give Gates command August 19 — two months before Burgoyne's surrender. But most historians feel that he deserves only a small part of the credit for the victory of Saratoga. Schuyler and others had made the preparations that led to victory: Gates got the credit even though he remained at his headquarters throughout the fighting, and all the battles were led by those fierce fighters Benedict Arnold and Daniel Morgan. When Gates did plan an attack, his plans had to be cancelled by an officer on the spot, because the British army was not where Gates thought it was. Gates also managed to quarrel with Arnold, his best fighting general, after the first of the 3 battles that led to Burgoyne's surrender. He relieved Arnold of command, and Arnold led the next battle with no official position, commanding by force of the troops' confidence in him. Arnold was wounded while leading a charge on the enemy lines: Gates, who could be petty and vindictive, refused to mention in his reports to Congress that Arnold had even been on the field of battle. He wanted all the credit for himself.

After Saratoga Gates spent much time lobbying in Congress: he wanted Washington's job. In June, 1780, he was given command of the American army in the south — what there was of it. Most of the American troops had been captured with Lincoln at Charleston. When Gates took command, he behaved arrogantly, ignoring the advice of his officers. He marched his small army of 3000 to attack the British, and arrived at the battlefield with his men ill-fed and exhausted. When 2200 British troops under Cornwallis attacked, Gates's ill-trained militia, who had been posted in the front line, broke and fled. The remaining third of the army fought bravely, but hopelessly, until they were destroyed. Alexander Hamilton commented, "His passion for Militia, I fancy will be cured, and he will cease to think them the bulwark of American liberty."

Gates fled with the militia instead of remaining with de Kalb's brave troops. He was riding a racehorse, which bore him 60 miles before night. In 3½ days after the battle, he got 200 miles away. Only 700 of his soldiers came together after the battle.

Gates did nothing more of significance in the war. After it, he was well known for his generosity to ex-soldiers — he had always had a reputation for being kind to the soldiers. When he moved to New York City in 1790, he freed his slaves and sold his Virginia estate. He died in 1806.

HORATIO GATES

Major General Baron de Kalb

Major General Baron de Kalb

When young Lafayette went to offer his services to the American cause to Silas Deane, the American representative in Paris, he took with him as interpreter an older soldier, the Baron de Kalb. De Kalb had risen by his talents. He began life in 1721 as Johannes Kalb, the son of a Bavarian peasant. At 16 he ran away from home; by 1743 he had promoted himself into the ranks of aristocracy and became a lieutenant in the French army. Over 6 feet tall and possessed of enormous strength and great physical endurance — he liked to walk 20 to 30 miles a day for fun — de Kalb rose without influence to the rank of Lieutenant Colonel in the French Army during the Seven Years' War. He was valued for his intelligence as well as his strength: after the peace in 1763, de Kalb was sent by the French foreign minister to the American colonies, to report on the likelihood that they would rebel against England at some future date.

When war broke out in America, de Kalb saw a chance to return to active service. He came to America with Lafayette. Congress, at first suspicious that he was another foreign adventurer, gave him a commission as a major general. Washington found his cheerful competence valuable during the cold winter of 1779-1780 at Morristown, and was impressed enough by de Kalb's prudent bravery to choose him to command a detachment of troops sent south to aid General Lincoln. De Kalb started south in April with one of the army's finest units, a group of Maryland and Delaware Continentals. Before they arrived, Lincoln surrendered his army in Charleston, and de Kalb's 1400 men became the American army in the south. They found little support there — no supplies, no food, no reinforcements. Congress decided that a foreign-born officer should not have such an important command, and sent General Gates, the victor of Saratoga, as head of the army. De Kalb did not resent his loss of command, and followed dutifully as Gates misled his small force to Camden, South Carolina.

In the battle of Camden, de Kalb commanded the right wing: his Maryland and Delaware Continentals were left on the field as the other 2/3 of the army fled at the first shots. Unable to see that they were alone on the field, de Kalb and his men fought on an hour. De Kalb's horse was shot, but his giant body could still be seen amidst his men. The British were among them: they fought with sabers, bayonets, clubbed muskets. All the British army attacked this last American force. De Kalb called for a bayonet charge: the Americans cut through the British, and turned to attack them again from the rear. They fought until none were left to fight, and de Kalb, bleeding from 11 wounds, fell. He died 3 days later. His skill and bravery deserved to be better used.

Major General John Sullivan

When the colonists began to make an army, few Americans had ever commanded many troops. Most of those who had had experience in the French and Indian Wars were now too old. So men were made generals by Congress who seemed to have a talent for leadership and definitely did have political backing in their own states. John Sullivan got his commission this way. Born in New Hampshire in 1740 of Irish parents, Sullivan was a successful lawyer and patriot leader there. He attended the First Continental Congress as a New Hampshire delegate, and impressed many with his energy, enthusiasm, and fighting spirit. He was always feisty: when he was not fighting the British, he was quarrelling with his friends and allies. Washington called Sullivan "active, spirited, and zealously attached

Major General John Sullivan

to the cause," but added that he was swayed by vanity and the desire to be popular, and lacked "the sound judgment and some knowledge of men and books" needed to overcome the "lack of experience . . . common to us all."

After serving with Washington at the siege of Boston, Sullivan was briefly in command of the army in Canada after Montgomery's death. He presided over its disorderly retreat as smallpox decimated it. He joined Washington again for the defence of New York. At the Battle of Long Island in August, 1776, Sullivan's command was surprised by Howe's flanking attack. They fell apart, and Sullivan was taken prisoner in a cornfield by 3 Hessians.

Exchanged, he was with Washington in the battles of Trenton and Princeton in December, 1776, where he led his troops bravely. But in September, 1777, when Washington was defending Philadelphia, Sullivan's troops were hit again by a surprise flanking attack at the battle of Germantown, after Sullivan had assured Washington that there was no danger of such an attack. The Americans were defeated, and part of the blame was Sullivan's.

The British occupied Newport, Rhode Island, which has an excellent harbor. A joint French and American expedition hoped to capture the 6000 British troops. Sullivan was given command of the American troops, and began his operation by quarrelling with the French Admiral, Comte d'Estaing. D'Estaing withdrew his fleet when a British fleet appeared, and Sullivan had to break off his siege and flee with his army. He accused everyone else of being responsible for the failure.

Sullivan had one more independent command, his most successful. It was decided that the Indians of the Six Nations, who were British allies, must be punished for their frontier raids. Washington ordered Sullivan to destroy the Indian towns and food supplies, and seize hostages. Sullivan led 5000 men through the Indian country. Because he was slow in starting, he lost his chance to surprise the Indians, and never captured any hostages. He did destroy a great many Indian houses, orchards, and crops ready to be harvested. The Indians suffered many discomforts from loss of food and homes. They were unable to attack the colonists as frequently that year; but their bitterness against them increased, and they attacked more fiercely in retaliation in the following years.

After this excursion Sullivan quarrelled with Congress, and resigned in a rage. After the war he was President of New Hampshire and later a district judge. He died in 1795.

Major General Baron von Steuben

In the winter of 1778 a European officer came to the American Congress. His name, he announced, was Frederick William Augustus Henry Ferdinand, Baron von Steuben, and he had served as a Lieutenant General under Frederick the Great of Prussia in the Seven Years' War. As Frederick's army had run rings around its larger opponents, von Steuben had an impressive background. (He had exaggerated his military and social rank to impress his audience: job-hunters often do.) But while many former European officers expected Congress to give them Washington's job, von Steuben only asked Congress to pay his expenses: he would serve as a volunteer, without rank or pay. Congress, impressed, sent him to Washington's winter quarters at Valley Forge, Pennsylvania.

Washington soon discovered that von Steuben was prepared to make himself useful. Although shocked that the troops lacked food, clothing, shelter, and even weapons and discipline, von Steuben was also impressed. He told Washington that no European army would have held together under such conditions.

Major General Baron von Steuben

Washington assigned von Steuben to instruct the troops in that Prussian system of drill and marching which had made Frederick the Great's army so successful. Such training makes a commander able to get his soldiers to do whatever is necessary — for example, forming a single line, facing the enemy — as quickly as possible without getting in one another's way. Von Steuben taught the army to march in rows of 4. Before his arrival they had marched single file, like Indians. Now a group of men covered only ¼ as much road: marches were finished more quickly. Von Steuben also showed the men how to move from marching order into line of battle, and how to shift that line of battle without disorder when an enemy came from a new direction. He also taught the men how to use their bayonets — which previously had been used mostly for roasting meat in camp. With the length of time reloading a musket took, and its great lack of accuracy, the bayonet was the surest weapon the men had.

Steuben began his lessons by working with a few men, while others watched. Then he worked with larger numbers, while yet more watched. His drill was the best show available at Valley Forge, partly because of Steuben's vigor and enthusiasm, partly because of his troubles with the language. He spoke only German and French, though he managed to memorize a few English commands and curses. When something went wrong, a stream of German and French curses flew across the field until the Baron remembered to call one of his aides, to whom he would say, "Come and swear for me in English." But Steuben was impressed with the intelligence of his American troops. He wrote a European officer, "You say to your soldier, 'Do this,' and he does it; but I am obliged to say, 'This is the reason why you ought to do that,' and then he does it."

By spring Steuben had remade the army, and he had the pleasure of seeing his students perform brilliantly at the confused battle of Monmouth. Washington was able to halt the American retreat because the troops had Steuben's training. Later Washington sent Steuben south with Nathanael Greene, saying, "There is an army to be created." Steuben drilled southern recruits, and was one of the officers singled out for praise by Washington after Yorktown. After the war Steuben was given land in upstate New York. He died in his log house in Steubenville in 1795, aged 64.

Colonel Alexander Hamilton

Alexander Hamilton's brilliant career began in the American Revolution. Born in the British West Indies in 1757, Hamilton was the illegitimate son of a Scottish merchant. He came to New York, and enrolled at King's College (now Columbia University). At 17 he was already a public speaker on the patriot side, and wrote political pamphlets as well in 1774 and 1775. He formed an artillery company made up of fellow students, and became its captain, serving in the battles of White Plains, Trenton, and Princeton.

Washington recognized the young man's brilliance, and took him onto his staff as a lieutenant colonel in March, 1777. Hamilton served until 1781 as Washington's chief secretary and unofficial chief of staff. He was invaluable to Washington, who said, "There are few men to be found of his age who has a more general knowledge than he possesses, and none whose soul is more warmly engaged in the cause, or who exceeds him in probity and sterling virtue." But Hamilton wanted a chance to win glory as a soldier in battle. When he left Washington's staff, he was given troops to command, and served under Lafayette at Yorktown, where Washington assigned him to lead an attack.

ALEXANDER HAMILTON

After Yorktown Hamilton left the army to become a New York lawyer. He married a daughter of General Philip Schuyler, and became a member of Congress, and a delegate to the Constitutional Convention. With James Madison he wrote the *Federalist* essays, which led many to support the adoption of the new Constitution. Under Washington Hamilton became the first U.S. Secretary of the Treasury, and the leader of the Federalist Party. In 1804 he was killed in a duel with Aaron Burr.

Major General Peter Muhlenberg

One of the best fighters in the American army was John Peter Gabriel Muhlenberg, a Lutheran minister. Born in Pennsylvania in 1746, the son of the founder of the Lutheran church in America, Muhlenberg was educated here and in Europe for the ministry. While in Germany, he served in the army in Anspach. A minister in Woodstock, Virginia, he was a representative to the Virginia House of Burgesses. In 1775 he preached his farewell sermon to his congregation, ending, "There is a time for all things; a time to preach and a time to pray, but those times have passed away; there is a time to *fight, and that time has come!*" Taking off his parson's gown, he revealed that he was wearing under it the uniform of a colonel. The drum was beaten at the church door for recruits, and nearly all the men in the congregation enlisted to fight with Muhlenberg.

He served at Charleston in 1776, and was made a Brigadier General in 1977. In May, 1777, he joined Washington, and fought with him at Brandywine, Germantown, and Monmouth. While attacking at Brandywine, Muhlenberg was recognized by the enemy troops — some of the Anspach jagers he had served with in his youth. They yelled out his old nickname, "*Hier commt Teufel Piet!*" ("Here comes Devil Pete!")

From 1779 through 1781 Muhlenberg fought in Virginia, and was back with Washington for Yorktown. At the end of the war he was promoted to major general. After the war Muhlenberg moved back to Pennsylvania where he served as a congressman, and later as a senator. He died in 1807.

Major General the Marquis de Lafayette

The American struggle for independence inspired the citizens of other countries while it was happening and in the years that followed. The Marquis de Lafayette, a wealthy young French nobleman, born in 1757, recently married to a beautiful girl whom he loved, gave up all his comforts. Opposing the orders of his king, he bought a ship, disguised himself as a postboy to evade arrest while reaching it, and crossed the Atlantic with 12 experienced officers, including Baron de Kalb, to aid the American cause. On leaving France, he wrote his wife that America was the hope of all humanity.

When Lafayette offered his services to Congress in July, 1777, they accepted his services as an unpaid volunteer, and made him a major general, as Silas Deane had committed them to do. They sent him to Washington, to serve as an aide. The two quickly became friends. Washington had no children; Lafayette's father had died while Lafayette was a child; they came to be almost father and son in their relationship. Lafayette made himself useful: at Brandywine he showed bravery under fire, continuing to rally retreating troops even after being wounded. He wanted to command troops — a problem, since his high rank would mean that he commanded more experienced officers. But his talents began to make the idea seem possible. De Kalb wrote home to France, "No one deserves

AN
une
APPEAL
appellation
TO
au
HEAVEN
ciel

a flag
of the war

more than he the esteem which he enjoys here. He is a prodigy for his age, full of courage, spirit, judgment, good manners, feelings of generosity, and of zeal for the cause of liberty." And Lafayette himself wrote his father-in-law, explaining the principles of conduct he was following: "I read, I study, I examine, I listen, I think, and out of all that I try to form an idea into which I put as much common sense as I can. I shall not speak much for fear of saying foolish things; I will risk still less for fear of doing them, for I am not disposed to abuse the confidence which they have deigned to show me."

Troops were willing to follow his lead, and Lafayette was given command of a division of Washington's army. As a commander of troops he was careful of his men's welfare, and even spent his own money to see them properly equipped. He learned his trade on the job, and, despite being always eager to fight, showed a caution which kept his mistakes from having serious results. He served well at Monmouth and at the abortive siege of Newport, then returned to France in 1779, to lobby for French troops to be sent to aid Washington.

When Lafayette returned, he was sent into Virginia in February, 1781. The British had sent the turncoat Benedict Arnold there to raid supplies, and Washington wanted Lafayette to capture Arnold for trial. But when Cornwallis brought his army into Virginia, Lafayette was heavily outnumbered. Now Cornwallis tried to capture him, but the young Marquis evaded his efforts. When Cornwallis under orders from his superiors retreated into the Yorktown peninsula, Lafayette was able to keep the British troops there until the arrival of the French fleet and the troops of Rochambeau and Washington trapped Cornwallis.

After Yorktown, Lafayette was made a major general in the French army. His ardor for freedom was unquenched: he suggested to Washington that the two of them should try to run a Virginia plantation with freed slaves as tenant farmers. Not everyone was free yet.

Lafayette's involvements in French politics kept him from returning to America. A popular hero in the early stages of the French Revolution, he was not extreme enough to satisfy the radicals who came into power, and whose bloody measures he loathed. Lafayette fled, and found himself in the hands of the Austrian government, for whom his ideas were too extreme. They kept him in prison for 3 years. While Napoleon ruled, Lafayette lived in retirement: he had not fought in America and France to see a monarch replaced by a military dictator. When Napoleon fell, Lafayette returned to politics, but was unable to see his republican ideas carried out. In 1824, invited by President Monroe, Lafayette returned to the United States — one of the last survivors of the Revolutionary commanders. He spent a year touring the country. Congress voted him $200,000 to restore a part of the fortune he had lost in various revolutions; 55 towns and countries were named for him; and everywhere he was received with joy as a living monument of the heroic past.

When the Bourbons were overthrown in 1830, Lafayette was offered the Presidency of a new French Republic, but he felt his country's people were not yet ready to rule themselves, and advised that a constitutional monarchy be established. He died in 1834, still inspired by the ideals of the American Revolution.

LAFAYETTE

ANTHONY WAYNE

Major General Anthony Wayne

"Mad Anthony" Wayne, as his troops called him, was born to be a soldier. As a schoolboy in Waynesborough, Pennsylvania, where he was born in 1745, he neglected his lessons to lead his friends in military games. After working as a surveyor, farmer, and tanner, he became active in politics just before the Revolution began, and was a leader in the local militia. And when the war started, he was one soldier who enjoyed his work.

He joined Washington's army for the battles around New York. In February, 1777, he was made a Brigadier General. At Brandywine he distinguished himself by hard fighting. But while commanding 1500 men who were operating close to the British rear, Wayne disregarded a warning that the British were after him, and let his men be surprised at Paoli, Pennsylvania, the night of September 20, 1777. The British bayonetted Wayne's sleeping men. Wayne felt disgraced after this "Paoli Massacre," and wanted revenge. He got it at Germantown October 4: his charge caught the British troops sleeping.

Wayne fought well again at Monmouth, but his most famous exploit of the war was the capture of Stony Point, a British stronghold on the Hudson below West Point. A peninsula protected on 3 sides by the Hudson, and on the fourth by a marsh and stream, Stony Point rose 150 feet above the river, and was fortified. After carefully scouting the position, Wayne led his brigade of light infantry, 1350 men, on a 13-mile secret march, and surprised the British with a bayonet attack. Led by axmen who cut a way through the fortifications, Wayne's men stormed the fort. Wayne was wounded, but told his men to carry him on into the fort. They took it and over 500 prisoners.

Wayne continued fighting throughout the war. At its end he was promoted to major general. When Washington needed a general to command an expedition against the Indians in 1794, he chose Wayne, and Wayne won a victory at the battle of Fallen Timbers. Wayne died in 1796.

When Washington was deciding to use Wayne against the Indians, he described him as "more active and enterprising than judicious and cautious," and worried about his vanity. Vain, impulsive, boastful, always eager to attack, occasionally careless — Wayne was all of these; but he was an exciting leader whom men would follow, a man who loved to fight, and whose aggressive instinct was valuable indeed in war.

Major General Nathanael Greene

Nathanael Greene has been called "the greatest military genius" of the American Revolution. Born in 1740 in Warwick, Rhode Island, Greene was brought up as an anchorsmith, with little education and no military background. He taught himself by reading at his forge. After serving at the siege of Boston, Greene became Washington's most trusted advisor, and was promoted to Major General. Too ill to fight during the battles around New York, Greene commanded a wing of the American army at Trenton, Princeton, Brandywine, and Germantown. In the Valley Forge winter of 1777-1778, over Greene's protests, Washington removed him from his troops and made him quartermaster General — the officer in charge of getting supplies to the troops. Despite a lack of money, supplies, and transportation, Greene's reorganized departments managed to get the army fed and clothed by spring.

But Greene wanted to command troops. When the news of Gates's defeat at Camden arrived, Congress asked Washington to select a general to take over in the south. Their choices, Lincoln and Gates, had failed. Washington sent Greene.

When Greene reached Charlotte, North Carolina, he found 1650 men. Half of them had no clothes or weapons. The British had almost complete control of Georgia and South Carolina, and only Greene's handful of men stood between them and North Carolina. Greene had to hold back the British while rebuilding his own army. He found a highly unorthodox way to do this. Usually generals are taught that a weaker army should never divide its forces when near a stronger enemy: the enemy can defeat each section in turn easily. But Greene decided to split his army in half. He would give the better troops to Daniel Morgan, who would go northwest of the British main army to harass them and stop their recruiting. Greene would take the rest of his army east of Cornwallis, to train and recruit. He would be 100 miles from Morgan, 75 from Cornwallis. If Cornwallis attacked either half, Greene relied on the greater speed with which an American army, unencumbered by much equipment, could move. Two small armies could attack Cornwallis in several places at once. Each would find it easier to feed itself in its area without eating the area bare. And whether Cornwallis attacked Morgan or Greene, he would leave the other force free to capture the British garrisons left behind him, and to cut off his supplies. Each small victory of this sort would deprive Cornwallis of part of his ability to get supplies from the area he had conquered.

Cornwallis saw Greene's plan, and tried to counter it. He sent a fast-moving force under Banastre Tarleton to attack Morgan, and moved his own main army into position to intercept the retreat of Morgan's defeated men. Morgan's victory at Cowpens upset his calculations, but Cornwallis decided to catch and destroy Morgan's army before they could rejoin the rest of Greene's men. To increase his men's speed Cornwallis destroyed many of his supplies, and burned his wagons. The 3 armies moved north as fast as they could — Morgan and Greene to join, Cornwallis to attack them separately. Greene had prepared for the possibility of such a campaign when he took command: he had ordered maps made of the North Carolina roads, and had built a fleet of boats for each of the rivers he might have to cross. North Carolina is divided by a series of rivers running roughly from east to west: winter rains frequently made them unfordable, and an army without boats could be trapped against a rising river, with no way to retreat. Cornwallis followed Morgan across 4 rivers, over roads of heavy red clay mud — the Broad, the Catawba, Lynch's Creek, and the Peedee. When Morgan and Greene finally joined, they still had only 2000 men to Cornwallis's 3000, and could not afford to fight him. The Americans had to cross the Yadkin and the Dan Rivers before they reached Virginia; with Cornwallis pressing behind them, driving his army as fast as any army has ever marched on some of the worst roads any army has ever covered. But Greene's ragged men stayed ahead. His rear guard operated on 3 hours' sleep a night, and 1 meal a day — they had no time to stop for more. In the last day, the rear guard covered 40 miles in 16 hours, and crossed the river at midnight. When Cornwallis arrived the Americans and their boats were all on the far side of the river.

Cornwallis now had to retreat back into North Carolina, hunting for supplies in country whose food had already been eaten. Greene followed him, to wear him down by constant skirmishing. As Greene's army increased in size, he decided to fight. He had 4400 men — although only 630 of them had ever fought before; Cornwallis had about 1900. They met March 15, 1781 at Guilford Court House. A bloody battle resulted, which

Major General Nathanael Greene

ended in a stalemate. In effect, however, the battle was an American victory. A quarter of Cornwallis's men were out of action, and he had to retreat to the sea at Wilmington to get supplies. Greene had reconquered North Carolina. Now he decided to start on South Carolina. Cornwallis, reduced to 1400 men, marched off to Virginia, hoping to draw Greene after him.

The British still had about 8000 men scattered in South Carolina and Georgia under Lord Rawdon. Greene found ways of attacking where he was stronger than they. He used the American guerilla leaders Marion, Pickens, and Sumter, and moved his army rapidly. Lord Rawdon with 900 troops attacked Greene with 1400 at Hobkirk's Hill near Camden April 25. The Americans were defeated, but the British were so weakened that they evacuated Camden. "We fight, get beat, rise, and fight again," said Greene cheerfully. Explaining his tactics, he said, "There are few generals that have run oftener, or more lustily than I have done. But I have taken care not to run too far, and commonly have run as fast forward as backward, to convince the Enemy that we were like a Crab, that could run either way."

After Hobkirk's Hill Greene divided his forces, and gobbled up a number of smaller British posts. Then came the final battle in the south, when Greene fought General Stuart at Eutaw Springs September 8, 1781, in one of the bloodiest battles of the war. The two sides were equally matched — the Americans had 2400 men, the British 2000. The Americans suffered from lack of equipment, as they had throughout the campaign. Many of the Continental infantry at Eutaw Springs had no coats, and had to tie pieces of Spanish moss "on the shoulder and flank to keep the musket and the cartridge-box from galling" their bare skin. The result was a standoff. But the British lost 40% of their army, and withdrew into Charleston, which they did not evacuate until December, 1782. In one year Greene had reorganized a defeated army, fought several battles, and regained most of the 3 southern states from an enemy superior in equipment, training, and number of men. He died in 1786 at his plantation near Savannah, which the state of Georgia had presented to him.

Brigadier General Daniel Morgan

At the beginning of the Revolution, Daniel Morgan hardly seemed likely to become a great general. Born in New Jersey of a Welsh family about 1735, he ran away from home at 17 to the western frontier of Virginia. A large, rough young man with enormous strength and little education, he became a teamster for Braddock's expedition against the French and Indians, then served as a soldier with a group of Virginia rangers. After the war he kept getting into trouble by spending more time in tavern brawls than in paying his debts. But when he took a common-law wife in 1763, he began to settle down.

At the start of the Revolution, Morgan raised a group of frontier scouts. His 96 riflemen went to join Washington in Boston: on foot they covered 600 miles in 3 weeks, a fair sample of the mobility which made them so valuable. When they marched through the Maine woods in Benedict Arnold's attack on Quebec, Captain Morgan's men broke trail for the expedition. And when Arnold was wounded in the assault on Quebec, Morgan took command, though other officers in the group had higher rank. He led the Americans on to a near success. When British troops surrounded the small party, Morgan wanted to fight their way out. Others decided to surrender. Morgan refused; weeping and raging, he stood with his back to a wall, waving his sword and daring any British soldier to come fight him for it. Finally he surrendered it to a passing priest, saying he would never yield it to such cowardly soldiers.

Brigadier General
Daniel Morgan

On his release from captivity, Morgan was promoted to Colonel, and assigned to command a corps of 500 light infantry, known as "Morgan's Rangers." They were sent to help fight Burgoyne, and were the most valuable American troops there. They made Burgoyne's scouts afraid to go into the woods, and thus useless. In the battle of Freeman's Farm, Morgan's men met the British in the woods as they were advancing to attack the American line: with Morgan in the woods, blowing his turkey-call as his rallying signal, the British never got to the lines. Morgan's men again played a major role in the battle of Bemis Heights, where Arnold and Morgan led the fighting.

In 1780 Morgan went south and joined Gates's defeated army. When Greene arrived, he had Morgan promoted to Brigadier General, and gave him command of half the army, operating to the northwest of Cornwallis. Cornwallis sent his ace cavalry commander, the dreaded Banastre Tarleton , to destroy Morgan. Tarleton had 1100 men, the pick of Cornwallis's army; Morgan had 1050, of whom half were militia. Usually the American militia ran away as soon as a battle began. Morgan planned to prevent that. He stopped to give his men a good night's rest, and picked a position carefully for his battle at Cowpens, South Carolina. He posted his men on a rising slope of ground. There was no place for them to retreat to: Morgan didn't want anything to give his militia that idea. He posted his steadiest troops, the 450 Continentals, at the crest of the rise in his third line. In front of them, lower down the hill, he put Colonel Andrew Pickens with his second line of 300 militia; and in the very front, a skirmish line of 150 picked riflemen. In reserve Morgan kept his 125 mounted men.

The night before the battle Morgan wandered among his men's campfires, stopping to talk with and inspire them. He made sure that not only every officer, but also every man, knew his plans for the battle: no one would run away in panic caused by misunderstanding. Morgan instructed his first two lines that each should fire two volleys once the British were 50 yards away, aiming at the officers. After that, they could retreat in an orderly fashion to behind the third line. As militia always ran when charged by British bayonets, Morgan made a virtue of necessity.

The battle began at 7 a.m. on January 16, 1781. The militia fired their volleys as ordered, staggering the British advance. William Washington's dragoons covered their retreat. Now the British and the Continental line engaged in a point-blank fight. The Americans stood up well for some time, then retreated to straighten their line. Tarleton thought he had the battle won, and his army charged forward. Morgan gave the command, and his Continentals faced about and delivered a volley that stopped the British in their tracks. Meanwhile Morgan ordered Washington's men to charge on the right, and the militia, now over their confusion, to charge on the left. The British were hit on both flanks in the classical military movement known as a double envelopment, which Hannibal had used at Cannae. British resistance folded; Tarleton fled the field. The British lost 9/10 of their force — 100 dead, 702 captured; Morgan lost 12 dead, 60 wounded. Within 2 hours after the battle ended, Morgan's army left Cowpens. They successfully evaded Cornwallis, and rejoined the rest of the American army. Morgan did not fight another battle: crippled by rheumatism, he was unable to serve in the field again. Greene felt his loss; as he said to his aides, "Great generals are scarce; there are few Morgans to be found." After the war Morgan served as a congressman. He died in 1802.

Brigadier General Thaddeus Kosciuszko

Thaddeus Kosciuszko was born in Polish Lithuania in 1736. After studying in the military school in Warsaw, he went on to study in France. Dr. Franklin recruited him for the American cause. Washington used Kosciuszko first as an aide. Then, discovering that his major talent lay in military engineering, a field in which most Americans had no experience, Washington set him to building fortifications and made him a colonel. In autumn, 1777, Washington sent Kosciuszko north to aid Gates against Burgoyne: he built the earthworks on Bemis Heights that stopped Burgoyne's advance. Later Kosciuszko fortified West Point. He also served in the south under General Greene, who valued his "sound judgment and engineering ability."

Kosciuszko's major glory came after the American Revolution. He was one of the many who, inspired by the American example, tried to free their own countries. In 1794 he led a revolution in Poland against its Russian conquerors. In October he was wounded, captured, and imprisoned in St. Petersburg until the death of the Empress Catherine the Great.

When Catherine died, her son Paul, who hated her, freed Kosciuszko, honored him, and offered him a post in the Russian army. Kosciuszko declined. The emperor offered to give Kosciuszko his own sword, and was answered, "I no longer need a sword, since I have no longer a country to defend." Kosciuszko died in exile in Switzerland in 1817.

Count Casimir Pulaski

Count Casimir Pulaski began fighting as a young man in his native Poland when his father led a rebellion in 1769 against King Stanislaus. After his father was captured and executed, young Casimir was elected leader of the rebellion. He and 39 of his companions attempted a daring feat in 1771: they entered Warsaw in disguise, intending to capture the King and take him to their army, to be a figurehead leader for their campaign against the invading Russian troops of Catherine the Great. They captured the King, but had to set him free again to escape from the city. Pulaski was outlawed in Poland, and joined the Turkish army in order to continue fighting the Russians.

Benjamin Franklin, our Ambassador in Paris, sent Pulaski over to join the American cause. A horseman capable of the most daring feats of skill, Pulaski began to organize some cavalry, an arm the Americans greatly needed. Mounted troops, the fastest-moving part of an army, were needed to watch the enemy's movements and report them in time for countermeasures to be taken. Cavalry could also move fast enough to be able to reinforce troops under attack and to attack the enemy's weak points. If Washington had had cavalry scouting his flanks at Long Island, that disaster could have been prevented.

After Pulaski's service at Brandywine, Congress made him a Brigadier General, and put him in charge of all the American cavalry. He resigned this post within a few months to form his own legion, a mixed command of cavalry and infantry. They fought at the battle of Germantown, and in February, 1779, Washington sent Pulaski and his men south to serve with General Benjamin Lincoln's army. Pulaski was killed there October 9, 1779, while leading a part of Lincoln's unsuccessful assault on Savannah, Georgia.

Brigadier General George Rogers Clark

George Rogers Clark commanded small armies, but achieved a great result. Born in Charlottesville, Virginia, in 1752, Clark became a surveyor and a lover of frontier life. He moved to Kentucky, which was just being settled as the Revolution began. The Indians resented the loss of their hunting grounds there, and, with the aid of arms supplied by British trading posts, attacked the American settlers. Clark decided that the best way to relieve Kentucky from these attacks was to capture the posts which supplied them. Virginia claimed to own that whole northwest territory under its colonial grant, so Clark went east across the mountains and persuaded Virginia's leaders to back his expedition. They gave him authority and money: Clark returned to Kentucky to raise his army. On June 26, 1778, he set out with his 175 men. To achieve surprise, they marched overland. On July 4 they arrived at Kaskaskia, Illinois. No one expected them, and they captured the post without a shot. Clark next took Cahokia, Illinois, and Vincennes, Indiana, also without a fight.

But the principal British post was in Detroit, and Clark did not have enough men to attack it. The commander in Detroit was called "Hamilton the Hair-Buyer" by the Americans, who believed that he paid the Indians for American scalps. When Hamilton heard of Clark's exploit, he led an army to Vincennes, and recaptured it. Clark, hearing this news, decided he would counterattack immediately, even though it was February. He wanted to retake Vincennes before the British had time to reinforce it strongly. He recruited some local settlers, most of whom were French: the area had only been captured from the French by the British at the end of the French and Indian War, and most of the inhabitants had no love for the British. He led his army of 127 men overland from Kaskaskia to Vincennes — 180 miles through lands flooded by winter. There were no animals to kill for food — the floods had driven them away. At times the men were up to their shoulders in icy water: one day they could only cover 3 miles. Their ammunition got wet. But they arrived.

At Vincennes the British had a fort commanded by Hamilton, who had nearly as many men as Clark. If anyone had known how weak Clark's force was, the citizens of the town and the local Indians would have joined Hamilton and exterminated Clark's army. Clark bluffed boldly: he rejected offers of aid from the French inhabitants and the Indians to convince them his army was so strong that he needed no help. They remained neutral. Clark attacked the fort, and Hamilton, impressed by his supposed strength, surrendered after a weak resistance.

Clark wanted to go on to attack Detroit, but never raised a large enough army. During the rest of the war he continued to protect Kentucky by fighting the Indians. He died in 1818.

Because of Clark's exploits, the Americans were able to claim the northwest territories in the peace treaty, and the new nation was not confined by the boundary of the Appalachian mountains. Its limits were later expanded further by the Louisiana Purchase, which was explored by the Lewis and Clark Expedition, one of whose leaders was George Rogers Clark's younger brother William.

Brigadier General
George Rogers Clark

JOANNI PAVLO JONES
CLASSIS PRAEFECTO.
COMITIA AMERICANA

Commodore John Paul Jones

America's first great naval hero was born John Paul in 1747, in Arbigland, Scotland. At 12 he was apprenticed and sent to sea. After having commanded his own ship, he settled in Virginia in 1773, and took the last name of Jones.

When the Revolution began, Congress made Jones senior lieutenant in the tiny new navy. He sailed with Commodore Esek Hopkins, then in 1777 was given command of the small *Providence*, with which he captured 15 prizes off the American coast. In November, 1777, he was given the larger *Ranger*, an 18-gun ship. He had the daring to cruise in the waters around the British Isles, taking his prizes in water the British thought they owned and even capturing a British town. His successes raised the cost of marine insurance for merchants, and lowered the British government's tax revenues. On April 24, 1778, Jones fought and captured the *Drake*, an English navy ship.

After this exploit, the King of France fitted out 5 ships for Jones to command. Their crews were of mixed nationality, and many of their officers were French, but the ships were officially American. Jones's flagship, a leaky old tub, was renamed the *Bonhomme Richard* (the French equivalent of the "Poor Richard" of Franklin's famous almanacs) in tribute to Dr. Franklin. When the small fleet began cruising, they captured 13 vessels. Jones had problems with Captain Landais of the *Alliance*, who would not obey his orders. On September 23, 1779, the fleet attacked a British convoy of 40 merchantmen bound for the Baltic, protected by 2 British navy ships, the *Serapis*, 44 guns, and the *Countess of Scarborough*, 22. About 7 at night Jones signalled his ships to attack: Landais again refused to obey orders, but the others complied.

Jones knew that the *Serapis* had more guns and better-trained gunners, so he laid his ship alongside her, and lashed the two ships together. From 8:30 to 10:30 the two ships fired into each other at point-blank range. Sharpshooters in the rigging fired their muskets, and grenades were tossed back and forth across the bloody decks. The *Richard* was leaking badly and slowly sinking. A panic-stricken officer released the prisoners held on the American ship so that they would not drown, and they surged onto deck, where they could have recaptured the ship; but Jones, seeing them, persuaded them that their only hope was to work the pumps. The British, seeing the desperate condition of Jones's ship, asked if he surrendered; he shouted back, "We have not yet begun to fight!"

The British were in bad shape too. Many of their men had been killed when a grenade blew up some ammunition. Their ship had been on fire 3 times. As the battle seemed stalemated, Jones's men saw the *Alliance* coming up to them, ready to enter the action for the first time. Expecting its aid, the Americans cheered. But Landais fired broadsides into both the *Serapis* and the *Bonhomme Richard*. His action has never been explained: some thought he was mad, others that he wanted Jones to be killed, so that he could capture the *Serapis* himself, retake the *Richard*, and claim credit for the whole victory. But in spite of his ally Jones captured the *Serapis*. The *Countess of Scarborough* surrendered then to another American ship.

Jones transferred his crew to the *Serapis*, and sailed her into port. The *Bonhomme Richard* sank 16 hours after the battle ended.

After the Revolution, Jones spent some time in France, then served a year as a Russian rear admiral. He died in France in 1792.

Major General Benjamin Lincoln

Major General Benjamin Lincoln

General Benjamin Lincoln served the American cause faithfully if unspectacularly throughout the war. Valued for his reliability, sober common sense, and business-like methods, Lincoln was never a dramatic soldier — just a fat, sleepy, lame Massachusetts deacon who never swore or raged. Born in Hingham in 1733, he served as the town clerk and colonel of the militia. He became president of the Massachusetts Provincial Congress, and was sent with some militia to join Washington after the retreat from New York City. He commanded Washington's right wing at the battle of White Plains, October 28, 1776. In February, 1777, after Washington had commended Lincoln as "an active, spirited, sensible Man," Congress made him a major general.

When Burgoyne's army was marching south from Canada, Washington sent Lincoln to command the militia being organized against him, hoping that Massachusetts men would turn out for the popular Lincoln. At Saratoga Lincoln was wounded in the ankle while reconnoitering.

In September, 1778, Congress chose Lincoln to command the Southern district. At this point Georgia had been recaptured by the British, and had returned to loyalty to the crown. Lincoln made a brave attack on Savannah with French aid, but did not capture it. Now the British attacked South Carolina. The state gave Lincoln little help in defending itself: the South Carolineans would not put their militia under Lincoln's orders, or let him draft their slaves to fight, or even lend their slaves to work on fortifications. Nor would they work themselves: because slaves did all physical work, South Carolineans looked down on labor. Despite his 224 saggy pounds, Lincoln worked on the fortifications with a shovel himself, hoping his example would inspire others.

When the British attacked, Lincoln yielded to the South Carolineans' insistance that Charleston be defended, and foolishly let his army be bottled up there. The British besieged the city, and the Charlestonians only gave Lincoln lukewarm support. He surrendered May 12, 1780, after a six-week siege. The Americans gave up 5400 men — the entire American army in the south. The British refused them the usual honors of war to show contempt for their weak defense and ragged condition.

After being exchanged, Lincoln returned to serve with Washington. He was present at Yorktown, where Washington imposed on the British the terms they had given Lincoln at Charleston, and directed Cornwallis's deputy to give his sword to Lincoln.

At the end of the war Lincoln became the first American secretary of war. He was chosen by Massachusetts to suppress Shay's Rebellion in 1787, which he did as bloodlessly as possible. He died in 1810.

FRANCIS MARION

Brigadier General Francis Marion

The best generals in the Revolutionary War found ways of fighting suited to the talents of their troops, the land in which they fought, and the means they had available, instead of attempting to follow European models of warfare. Francis Marion of South Carolina, who practiced guerilla warfare before that name was invented, made brilliant use of his limited means to produce great damage to the British.

Marion was born in South Carolina in 1732 of French Huguenot ancestry. He had some military experience before the Revolution, fighting Indians, then served as a major in Moultrie's regiment at Fort Sullivan. He also fought at the unsuccessful assault on Savannah. Unable to serve because of a broken ankle, he was not in Charleston when his regiment surrendered there.

Marion raised a small command of twenty men, and offered their services to General Gates. The men were ragged and ill-equipped; Marion was small and unimpressive. Gates told them to go home, he had no need for them. Thus Marion had the good fortune to miss the battle of Camden.

He returned to his district with his men, and started independent operations. After Camden he and 16 of his men captured a detachment of British troops who were escorting 160 American prisoners, and freed the prisoners. This operation typified Marion's style: "The Swamp Fox" attacked fast, surprised his foe, achieved his purpose, and got away again into his swamps before his enemies could concentrate their superior forces to crush him. His command varied in number from hundreds to a dozen ragged black and white men. Their principal headquarters were at Snow's Island, at the junction of Lynch's Creek and the Peedee River, amid the swamps. There the sympathetic citizens of the area brought information about British positions. Marion's men had great effect on British movements: since they might suddenly appear anywhere, all British supplies had to be escorted by enough troops to withstand a strong attack, and all British-occupied towns had to have large, alert garrisons. The British then either had to use up all their troops in convoys and garrisons, which kept them unable to field a large army against Greene's, or else lose their supplies and other benefits from the area they had conquered.

General Greene fully appreciated the value of these guerilla operations, and made use of Marion and his colleagues Thomas Sumter and Andrew Pickens. Often Greene reinforced Marion with Lee's Legion: Lee and Marion conducted several highly successful operations together. When they lacked the equipment for a job, they invented another method. At Fort Watson, for example, they were facing a garrison in a strong stockade, and had no artillery with which to knock down the walls. By night they constructed a tower higher than the stockade, and placed riflemen in it. The sharpshooters were able to kill British troops trying to protect the walls from attack: the garrison surrendered.

Because of his inventiveness and activity as a general, and the feats he performed with small forces, legends collected about Marion. He seemed a Robin Hood of the swamps. Marion himself was a soft-spoken man, scrupulous about treating his enemies well, who never talked of his exploits after the war. He died in 1795.

Lieutenant Colonel Henry Lee

Henry Lee of Virginia became known as "Light-Horse Harry" by his active, daring management of his mixed legion of infantry and cavalry, "the most thoroughly disciplined and best equipped scouts and raiders in the Revolution."

Born in Virginia in 1756, Lee went to Princeton University. He joined the army in 1776, and joined Washington in September, 1777. His most famous exploit of the war was the capture of Paulus Hook in 1779. This British fortified post was a peninsula, now a part of Jersey City. Lee's men made a long march, achieved surprise after wading through water chest-deep, and successfully conducted a difficult and dangerous retreat with their prisoners.

But Lee's most valuable service was in the American army in the south. Washington sent Lee south with Nathanael Greene, and Lee's Legion seldom had an idle day till the end of the war. Often they operated with Francis Marion, emerging from the swamps to surprise the British. Often they served as Greene's scouts, or gathered his supplies. But all these other services never left them unready for battle, and they fought ferociously, missing none of Greene's battles. Lee and William Washington's men were "constantly kept on the alert, never stationary," in incessant activity. They continued to serve until the end of the war.

After the war Lee was a congressman and Governor of Virginia. He wrote memoirs of the war, and was chosen by Congress to speak George Washington's funeral oration: it was Lee who called his former commander, "First in war, first in peace, first in the hearts of his countrymen." In 1814 Lee was wounded while suppressing a riot in Baltimore. He died 4 years later, leaving a son who was to be an even greater general — Robert E. Lee.

Lieutenant Colonel William Washington

William Washington, called "the sword of his country," was one of the most effective American cavalry commanders. Born in Virginia in 1752, he was educated for the church, but became a soldier instead when the Revolution began. He served with his distant kinsman George Washington, beginning with the battles around New York City. At Trenton Captain William Washington and his fellow-Virginian, Lieutenant James Monroe, were the only officers wounded. He also fought at Princeton, then was sent south where the more open terrain gave more power to cavalry. After serving with Lincoln at Charleston, Washington was with Nathanael Greene on his great southern campaign. Washington's men served with distinction with Morgan at Cowpens, and covered the rear of Greene's army during his retreat across North Carolina to the Dan River. They returned with Greene to fight at Guilford Court House, Hobkirk's Hill, and Eutaw Springs. Between battles they were incessantly active, screening the movements of Greene's army from enemy observation and gathering all sorts of information about the enemy's movements. Washington was wounded and captured at Eutaw Springs when his horse was killed; he remained a prisoner till the end of the war. He then settled in South Carolina, where he died in 1810. Known for his taciturnity, Washington declined to become governor of South Carolina on the grounds that he could never make a speech.

Commodore Joshua Barney

Joshua Barney had the unusual distinction of being a hero in both the Revolutionary War and the War of 1812. Born in Baltimore in 1759, Barney went to sea as a boy. At 14 he was a second mate, at 16 he had his first command. When the Revolution began, young Barney was commissioned a first lieutenant in the navy. In 1780, as lieutenant on the sloop-of-war *Saratoga*, Barney led the boarding party of 50 men that captured the brig *Charming Molly*. He was appointed to command the prize, and brought her safely back to port. Barney then took command of the *Hyder Ally*, commissioned by the state of Pennsylvania, a small ship with 110 men, and in 1782 fought one of the most famous naval actions of the war. While cruising to destroy British privateers in the Delaware, he encountered the British sloop-of-war *General Monk*. Although the *General Monk* was stronger than the *Hyder Ally*, and although several other British ships were nearby, Barney attacked, and captured her in half an hour in what the historian of the U.S. navy called "one of the most brilliant actions that ever occurred under the American flag." The proud Americans sang:

> Come all ye lads that know no fear,
> To wealth and honor we will steer
> In the *Hyder Ally* privateer,
> Commanded by bold Barney.

Barney was given command of the *General Monk*, and sailed her to France. When he was received at court, Queen Marie Antoinette and her ladies in waiting kissed the handsome young sailor to congratulate him for his victory — at least, that was the reason they gave. Now another song was written about Barney — "Barney, Leave the Girls Alone!" On his return voyage Barney brought the news of the signing of the peace with Britain.

Barney stayed in the navy till 1793, when he resigned in disgust at having some shore sailors promoted over him. He entered the French navy, and commanded 2 French frigates. Leaving the French service in 1802, he returned to the U.S. navy in 1812 to participate in the new war against Britain. During the first year of the war he captured 15 prizes and sank 9 more. Kept in port by the British blockade, he improvised a squadron of small boats in Chesapeake Bay and harassed the British fleet there. In 1814, when British troops attacked Washington, Barney blew up his ships to avoid having them captured, and marched his 500 seamen inland to help defend the capitol. He armed his men with navy cannon from the Navy Department in Washington, and marched out to Bladensburg, arriving at the beginning of the battle. The American militia fled at the first British shot, leaving only Commodore Barney and his seamen to stand off the British army. They stood and fought at the District of Columbia line, holding back the British for some time and inflicting considerable damage. When the British began to surround his men, Barney ordered them to retreat. He was wounded in the hip, and captured, but the British, who admired his bravery, treated him well. He died in Pittsburg — an unlikely place for a sailor — in 1818, having survived 17 battles in the Revolutionary War, 9 in the War of 1812.

HYDER-ALI CAPT. JOSHUA BARNEY 1782

Lieutenant General Comte de Rochambeau

When the French government allied itself with the American rebels against the British, it decided to send troops to help the Americans. To command this force they chose Lieutenant General Jean Baptiste Donatien de Vimeier, Comte de Rochambeau, a veteran soldier. Rochambeau, who was born in 1725, had served in the French army since he was 16. He and his troops arrived in Newport, Rhode Island, in the summer of 1780.

In 1781 Washington sent a detachment of his army to Virginia under Lafayette's command to capture the traitor Benedict Arnold, who was leading raids there. Shortly after Lafayette arrived, Cornwallis brought his army north from North Carolina, hoping to cut off the flow of supplies from Virginia to Greene's army in the south. Clinton, the British supreme commander in New York, ordered Cornwallis to concentrate his troops at a seaport so that they could be transported to New York, since Clinton feared that Washington and Rochambeau would join to attack New York.

Now Washington and Rochambeau saw a chance for a major stroke against Cornwallis. If two French fleets, that of Admiral de Grasse in the West Indies, and that of Admiral de Barras in Newport, could join in Chesapeake Bay without either fleet being destroyed on the way by the British, then they would be stronger than the British fleet in the new world, and could prevent Cornwallis's evacuation. If Lafayette could keep Cornwallis pinned against the ocean, and if Washington and Rochambeau could bring their troops to Virginia quickly, without Clinton realizing their intentions, they would have more men than Cornwallis. The plan relied on a great many "if's" and no one was more conscious of its risks than Washington. But his army was dwindling, Congress was unable to raise money to pay them or buy them supplies, and without an American success, the American cause might wither away.

The French and American troops managed their march south flawlessly. Clinton was completely deceived. When Rochambeau and his staff arrived by boat at Chester, Pennsylvania, they were amazed to see on the dock the normally dignified Washington jumping up and down, waving a handkerchief, and shouting at them: Washington had just heard that the French fleet had arrived safely in Chesapeake Bay. When Rochambeau landed, Washington embraced him: after years Washington could see at last the prospect of a major victory.

The French fleet managed to preserve command of the sea off Yorktown against a badly handled British relief attempt. Cornwallis was trapped by a superior army, and the result was inevitable. After a 13-day siege Cornwallis surrendered October 19, 1781, giving up nearly 7000 troops who marched out with their bands playing "The World Turned Upside Down." Although the war did not end for another two years, this victory led to its end. The British did not reinforce their troops in America, and no more major battles took place.

Yorktown could not have been won without the French fleet and the French army. Their equipment and skill in siege warfare were invaluable.

Rochambeau returned to France in 1782, and was made a field marshal. He commanded an army at the beginning of the French Revolution, but was taken from command as politics became more radical. Arrested by Robespierre, he survived to be pensioned by Bonaparte. He died in 1807, aged 82.